Wednesdays With Wooden

A doctor's house calls and his unique
bond with a legendary coach

DR. MICHAEL LEVI

With Larry Stewart

FriesenPress

Suite 300 - 990 Fort St

Victoria, BC, V8V 3K2

Canada

www.friesenpress.com

ISBN
978-1-4602-8417-9 (Hardcover)
978-1-4602-8418-6 (Paperback)
978-1-4602-8419-3 (eBook)

1. BIOGRAPHY & AUTOBIOGRAPHY, SPORTS

Distributed to the trade by The Ingram Book Company

Table of Contents

Introduction

In the spring of 2008, I received a call on my cell phone while coaching my son's little league team. I wasn't supposed to use my phone in the dugout, but this call was from my father.

I left the dugout to take the call and told the other manager I'd be right back.

"What's up Dad?" I asked.

"Michael, do you have a moment?"

Since I detected an unusual tone in his voice, I asked again what was up.

"Michael, I have cancer," he said bluntly.

I remember my father had complained of lower back pain several weeks earlier, and he went to his internist for a check-up. Initially, his doctor didn't think much of it, but a follow-up with a specialist determined it was serious. My dad recited numerous numbers.

My heart sank.

Being a doctor, I knew what those numbers meant. My father, the person I loved and I admired more than anyone in the world, the person who had centered and guided my life, had pancreatic cancer.

The years to follow were difficult but we plowed through good times and not so good times. The love for him never changed, and that is why this book is dedicated to my late father.

When I was a small boy, my father introduced my sister and me to sports. He played tennis throughout his life, and basketball and football in his younger days. Sports were a big part of our family life. My dad took us to football, basketball and baseball games. However, what he enjoyed most was UCLA basketball. He'd marvel at the teachings of Coach John Wooden and sometimes he'd leave work early so we could attend a practice together.

It was from this nurturing and my father's admiration from afar that I first learned about Coach Wooden. Beginning in 2002, I got to know the Coach personally through visits to his home as his podiatrist, generally on Wednesdays.

Wednesdays With Wooden is mostly a compendium of notes that I wrote after those visits. This is not another John Wooden biography. Plenty of those have been written. My aim with this book is to provide a little more insight into this legendary sports figure through my personal experiences.

Writing the book first occurred to me when I began making the house calls to the Coach's home. I thought of Mitch Albom's 1997 wonderful best-seller, *Tuesdays With Morrie*, about the author's home visits with an old college professor who was dying of Lou Gehrig's disease. Thus the title of this book.

After I began medically treating Coach Wooden, my house calls, at least the medical aspect, were almost secondary to the stories I learned and the people I met. My dad, who got to know the Coach through me, enjoyed spending time with his hero. It was gratifying as his son to be able to give back to my father, who was always so supportive of me.

Maybe it was my father's own childhood that made him the way he was. His mother died in a car accident when he was 2. He spent his high school years in boarding school. Then his father passed away when he was 23. He seemed bound and determined to be the best father he could be – and he was, all the way up until his death in 2010.

At my father's funeral, my eulogy included this passage:

"You were a wonderful dad and even though you were proud of me, I was even more proud that you were my father."

For this book project, I used a Dictaphone to record recaps of my conversations with the Coach, particularly during the first couple of years of our relationship. A friend transcribed the tapes for me, and I printed out copies for safe keeping. But the transcribed material got put away, and for several reasons, the book idea got shelved along with my notes.

Then during the 2014-15 basketball season, Chris Erskine, the excellent, multi-purpose columnist for the *Los Angeles Times*, wrote about me, mainly because of my job as team podiatrist for the Los Angeles Clippers. I think what piqued Erskine's interest in me was that I purchased jerseys, got them autographed by Clipper players and coaches, and delivered them to Children's Hospital of Los Angeles.

I told Erskine about my relationship with Coach Wooden and my book idea. I also mentioned that I needed someone to help me write it. He connected me with a former *Times* colleague, Larry Stewart, who became my co-author.

Wednesdays With Wooden

Chapter 1:
The Beginning, Starting with the Feet

In the latter part of John Wooden's life, I was his podiatrist. But that does not mean I will be writing much about his feet, nor will I be spending a lot of time rehashing the feats that established him, according to many experts, as the greatest coach in any sport during the 20th century.

If you're reading this book, you likely know about his 10 national championships in a 12-year span as UCLA's basketball coach and his team's many other accomplishments, such as winning 88 straight games in the early 1970s.

This is my personal story about conversations with the legendary John Wooden during many visits to his home in Encino, California. The topics included basketball, poetry, family and more.

In this case, I was a doctor who made house calls. In doing so, I got to know a man I had always admired and respected from afar. He would become a father figure, and almost as dear to me as my own late father.

There were plenty of similarities between the two. Like the Coach, my father, Myron "Mike" Levi, had Midwestern values—hard working, competitive, gentle, caring and humble.

Both were good athletes, though I would not put my father in the same athletic class as the Coach, who is one of only three men in the Basketball Hall of Fame as both a player and a coach. Bill Sharman and Lenny Wilkins are the other two. The Coach was also outstanding in baseball and other sports as well. He once had a hole in one and a double eagle in the same round of golf—an almost unbelievable feat.

My father was a halfback on the football team at the University of Wisconsin in Madison and was always active. He played tennis throughout his life and was always involved in a variety of sports.

Both were successful in their chosen professions, my father in the banking and financial world; the Coach in coaching, or what he preferred to call "teaching."

They both died in 2010, my father on March 23 at the age of 82, the Coach on June 4 at the age of 99.

I grew up not far from Pauley Pavilion. As a small boy I would go to every UCLA game, sit high in the rafters, and watch the basketball team. My father would put me on his knee and point to the small men on the basketball court—they were small from our vantage point. He would talk to me about Coach Wooden and how important he was to the team, and how much he admired his wisdom and teachings.

As I grew older, I began to grasp that I was witnessing sports history. This was around the time UCLA began its amazing run of 10 national championships in 12 years, spanning from the 1963-64 season until the Coach's retirement at the end of the 1974-75 season.

I became an avid fan, and loved going to Pauley. When I went with a friend, my parents allowed us to walk around the arena and sometimes we would sneak down the stairwell, get by the security guards and greet the players when the horn sounded at the end of the game.

Occasionally we would build up the nerve to ask for a sweatband or an autograph. Then, after most of the crowd had filed out of the arena, we would walk onto the floor. If we were able to sneak a basketball into the arena, we would shoot around for a few minutes, pretending to be Lynn Shackelford, Kenny Heitz or one of the other players.

In the summers I attended a number of Coach Wooden's day camps. They took place over two weeks at nearby Palisades High School. The camps drew some 200 to 300 kids from grades 3 through 11. Besides the Coach, assistants such as Denny Crum, Frank Arnold and Gary Cunningham would be there, along with high school coaches such as Bud Ware of Taft and Jerry Marvin of Palisades.

When we arrived in camp, we were given a 30-page single-spaced Player's Notebook, which contained the Coach's Pyramid of Success, some of his favorite passages and sayings, and detailed instructions on fundamentals.

I saved my notebook, which remains in good condition today. In the introduction, the Coach emphasizes physical condition, proper and quick execution of the basic fundamentals and teamwork.

One page includes a passage titled "Press On." In part, it reads, "Nothing can take the place of persistence . . . talent will not . . . genius will not . . . education will not . . . persistence and determination alone are omnipresent."

A section on free throws, for example, contained 11 key rules a player should follow. Rule No. 9 is one example. It states: "Do not worry about a missed free throw. Your percentage of making the next one increased with every one you miss, provided you do not worry."

At the day camp that I attended, Coach Wooden had us do the same thing he had his UCLA players do on the first day of practice. He would have us sit down on the gym floor and take off our shoes and socks. He would then demonstrate how to properly put on our socks and then our shoes.

He would explain how important this was in order to prevent blisters or any other foot problems. It was my introduction to podiatry, the care of the human foot. I had no idea at the time that this would end up as my life's work.

At the age of 12 in 1971 I went to the Coach's weeklong sleep-away camp at Cal Lutheran. What an experience this was.

It wasn't just being around basketball, a sport I had grown to love, or being around Coach Wooden, the man I admired so much. I also got to be around the Dallas Cowboys, whose pre-season training camp was at the same facility. Many a morning we would all sit together, the basketball campers and the Dallas Cowboys, in the same cafeteria. Although not able to appreciate that much at the time, I was rubbing shoulders with the likes of Roger Staubach, Bob Lilly and Calvin Hill.

At these camps Coach Wooden would go over the fundamentals of dribbling and passing. He would come to each camper's side and watch them do calisthenics and drills. As a young boy I found his presence intimidating, and yet I remember him being very sincere. It was obvious to me that he took a special interest in all of us.

Towards the end of the camp we took the ceremonial picture. All the campers would wear their camp T-shirt and sit with Coach Wooden for a personal photograph. There were hundreds of campers, yet the Coach would make time to sit for a snapshot with each of us. In the ensuing years I treasured my photo, me in my horn-rimmed glasses posing with the legendary coach.

During the seventh and eighth grade I played on my school teams and watched basketball for many, many hours. At this point of my life, academics were not very important to me. I was more interested in basketball and sports in general. This continued through my freshman year of high school. I still was not much of a student and my report cards were mostly populated with C's and even an occasional D. Yet in the back of my mind, I always wanted to go into medicine.

As my 10th grade year approached, I was to meet with my high school counselor, Mr. Carlin. It was an important day, particularly since this was the time students decided which colleges to apply to. By planning ahead, I had the time to work on a strategy and to select the appropriate courses.

In the meeting with Mr. Carlin, he asked where I would like to go to college. I immediately responded, "Either UCLA or UC Santa Barbara."

My counselor looked at my grades, paused and said, "Perhaps a junior college would be more appropriate, such as Santa Monica College, which is near our school." He added, "You don't have the grades."

He also asked what field I would be interested in. I said I had aspirations to be a doctor. He said that would be fine, but a career in another aspect of medicine might be more fitting considering my poor grades.

At the end of the session I walked out of the counselor's office somewhat downcast. I went home and sat at my desk, where I had hung the Pyramid of Success from my Player's Notebook. I looked at it and observed the building blocks. The one at the top was titled "Competitive Greatness" and included this passage: "Be your best when your best is needed."

Other blocks of the pyramid dealt with such topics as industriousness, friendship, loyalty, cooperation, and enthusiasm.

I studied the entire pyramid, and this became a daily routine until I had it fully memorized. Before doing my schoolwork I would study the building blocks, going from the top to the bottom, then from the bottom to the top.

The pyramid became my guiding light, and I am convinced it made me a better, more devoted student. I now had a game plan for what I wanted to do with my life, and I had a guide to help me achieve my goals.

The C's became mostly A's and I ended up going to UC Santa Barbara.

I continued to work hard and continued my goal of practicing medicine by attending the Ohio College of Podiatric Medicine in Cleveland.

My parents Mike and Ursula, with me when I graduated from podiatry school.

Chapter 2:
A Breakfast Meeting

I was drawn to podiatry because I became an avid runner. To a runner, healthy feet are a priority.

After completing my schooling, I started my own podiatry practice on the third floor of a medical building in Santa Monica, California. On my office desk is the Pyramid of Success, which took Coach Wooden 15 years to create. Adjacent to the Pyramid is the picture of Coach Wooden and me at his Cal Lutheran camp.

One day in 1991, I went downstairs to get my mail. As the door of the elevator opened, a thin gray-haired blue-eyed man looked at me and nodded. "Good day," he said. It was none other than John Wooden. He was headed up when the elevator stopped on my floor. Suddenly, going downstairs to get the mail wasn't that important, and I went up on the elevator instead.

I shook John Wooden's hand and said, "Hello, I'm Dr. Michael Levi and it is a pleasure to meet you." I was in awe as I attempted to tell the Coach how much I had always admired him.

We rode up to the seventh floor, where he was going to visit Dr. Roderick Turner, a doctor for the UCLA basketball team during the Wooden era who is also a friend of mine. Before getting off the elevator, the Coach thanked me and said goodbye.

I went back downstairs to get the mail and then returned to my office.

"Wow," I thought. "I can't believe what just happened."

That afternoon I got the Coach's address from my friend, Dr. Turner. I sent a letter to the Coach, along with the photo of him and me that was taken when I was 12 years old.

A few weeks later, I got a wonderful reply. The Coach wrote on the photograph, "*Thank you, Michael, for your interest*," and added his signature.

He also included a note on his personal stationary that read: "*The photo seems to reveal the fact that both of us have matured somewhat. Best wishes, sincerely John Wooden.*"

*Here's that photo of me at age 12 with the
Coach. He signed it for me years later.*

Eleven years later, in 2002, Dr. Turner's wife had a serious foot problem and became my patient. Fortunately, I was able to take care of it.

Dr. Turner, in thanking me profusely, said, "Is there anything I can do for you?"

I said, "As a matter of fact there is. I'd love to have a visit with John Wooden, something more than an elevator conversation."

Dr. Turner delivered by setting up a breakfast. I asked if I could invite my father and Dr. Turner said, "Of course."

I woke up early on the designated day, a Friday morning. I got dressed not knowing what to expect, but certainly excited. My father came to my house and we drove to Dr. Turner's home in Pacific Palisades, picked him up at 7 a.m., and then made the 35-minute drive to the condominium building where Coach Wooden lived. After buzzing the Coach's unit, he opened the gate so we could get to his second-floor condominium. We were met at the door by UCLA athletic trainer Tony Spino, who assisted the Coach in his daily life for years.

The Coach had just finished his early morning workout and greeted us as we entered his home. He wasn't quite ready, so Dr. Turner gave us a short tour of the two-bedroom unit. In the room was a small double bed where the Coach slept. The bed also served as a shrine to his late wife Nell, who died in 1985. On her side of the bed was a large pillow embroidered with her name.

In the study were numerous team pictures. On one wall was his college Hall of Fame plaque. His table was full of books of all types, and there was reading material everywhere. A lot of people, like me, admired Coach Wooden. He also had people he admired as well, namely Abraham Lincoln and Mother Theresa. There was evidence of that throughout his home in the way of books and photos. His study was small, and the walls were also dominated with photos, championship trophies and plaques. Most of the photos were of former players and family members. Bookshelves lined the walls from the hallway to the small kitchenette adjacent to the living room. His desk was full of letters and packages from people seeking his signature. I would learn later that he always obliged until they finally became too much for him. It was also expensive, as it was rare for people to send return postage.

We sat down and began to talk.

My father, being very gregarious, started the conversation by asking the Coach about his early years in Indiana. Coach Wooden said that his father was very strict. For instance, he prohibited swearing. He said his father, who often read aloud to him and his older brother Maurice, believed that reading was a necessity in leading a fruitful life.

My father told Coach Wooden that he, as a youth, had spent summers on an uncle's farm in Indiana, where, among other things, there was no inside bathroom. Coach Wooden and my father laughed about some of the hardships, such as using the Sears-Roebuck catalog as toilet paper.

After some more conversation we decided it was time to leave for breakfast. We all went in my car to the Coach's favorite place for breakfast, VIP's on Ventura Boulevard in nearby Tarzana.

Toward the end of the breakfast, I was telling the Coach about my profession and what I did for my patients in the way of foot care. He said he needed a podiatrist, and he asked if I would consider serving that role.

"I'd be honored," I responded.

He said there was one catch. "You'll need to come to my home," he said.

Suddenly his offer sounded even better.

When we got back to his place, we said goodbye. The Coach thanked us for coming and gave us both hugs.

As I drove home I was beaming while thinking about all the great memories I now had. And I knew that with John Wooden now being a special patient of mine, there would be many more to come.

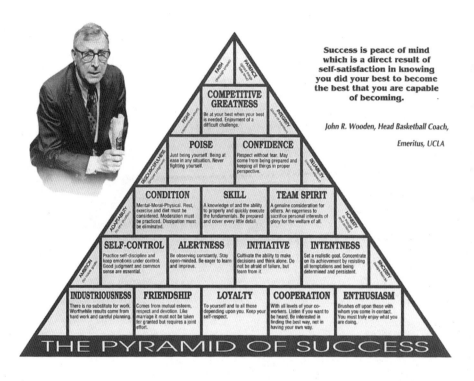

Success is peace of mind which is a direct result of self-satisfaction in knowing you did your best to become the best that you are capable of becoming.

John R. Wooden, Head Basketball Coach,

Emeritus, UCLA

COMPETITIVE GREATNESS
Be at your best when your best is needed. Enjoyment of a difficult challenge.

POISE
Just being yourself. Being at ease in any situation. Never fighting yourself.

CONFIDENCE
Respect without fear. May come from being prepared and keeping all things in proper perspective.

CONDITION
Mental-Moral-Physical. Rest, exercise and diet must be considered. Moderation must be practiced. Dissipation must be eliminated.

SKILL
A knowledge of and the ability to properly and quickly execute the fundamentals. Be prepared and cover every little detail.

TEAM SPIRIT
A genuine consideration for others. An eagerness to sacrifice personal interests of glory for the welfare of all.

SELF-CONTROL
Practice self-discipline and keep emotions under control. Good judgment and common sense are essential.

ALERTNESS
Be observing constantly. Stay open-minded. Be eager to learn and improve.

INITIATIVE
Cultivate the ability to make decisions and think alone. Do not be afraid of failure, but learn from it.

INTENTNESS
Set a realistic goal. Concentrate on its achievement by resisting all temptations and being determined and persistent.

INDUSTRIOUSNESS
There is no substitute for work. Worthwhile results come from hard work and careful planning.

FRIENDSHIP
Comes from mutual esteem, respect and devotion. Like marriage it must not be taken for granted but requires a joint effort.

LOYALTY
To yourself and to all those depending upon you. Keep your self-respect.

COOPERATION
With all levels of your co-workers. Listen if you want to be heard. Be interested in finding the best way, not in having your own way.

ENTHUSIASM
Brushes off upon those with whom you come in contact. You must truly enjoy what you are doing.

THE PYRAMID OF SUCCESS

Chapter 3:
The Treatments Get Underway

The first time I treated the Coach at his home was a warm August day in 2002. It was only a couple of weeks after my father, Dr. Turner and I had breakfast with the Coach.

I must admit I was a bit nervous. It was surreal that this was coming to fruition. At the breakfast he had asked me about coming to his home to treat his feet, but I wasn't sure it was going to happen until we talked later on the phone.

I arrived first thing in the morning and knew the drill. I parked in one of the visitor spots outside the main garage, walked over to the mailboxes where buzzers for each unit were located and looked for No. 101.

The name Wooden appeared above the number, as if he was just another one of the tenants. As I would learn, he wouldn't have wanted it any other way.

When I pressed the button for unit 101, the Coach buzzed me in. I took an elevator up one flight, and as the door opened he was there to greet me.

After entering his condo, I was pleasantly surprised to see a massage table set up at the foot of his bed. I had been in such awe during my first visit I had forgotten it was there. The bedroom was small, so it was a tight squeeze, but I had enough room and the massage table gave me a place to work.

I asked the Coach to take off his shoes and socks, which was kind of ironic. My first experience with the Coach many years earlier had been when he showed all of us campers how to put on our socks and shoes.

I checked his feet over, observed the circulation in his feet, checked his deep tendon reflexes and range of motion, and looked for any skin irritations. This and more became my routine, which also included treating corns, trimming his nails, and providing palliative care. At this point in his life, arthritis had already racked his body, including his feet.

I asked him what kind of exercise he does. He told me he gets physical therapy, and added, "That's about it. However, Dr. Levi, I don't think that really helps very much."

He always called me Dr. Levi. I thought it was too formal, but I knew that was what he preferred.

The newspaper headlines around this time in August of 2002 were the passing of the Lakers' legendary announcer Chick Hearn. He died on August 5, three days after taking a fall at his home in Encino, about three miles southeast of the Coach's condo. Chick was outside by his pool attempting to move a large plant when he slipped and hit his head on the concrete. The funeral was held August 9 at a church in Brentwood.

"Did you know Chick very well?" I asked the Coach. "Did you go to his funeral?"

He said he went with Kareem Abdul-Jabbar, the former UCLA center then known as Lew Alcindor who later became the NBA's all-time leading scorer while with the Lakers. "He picked me up," the Coach said.

Our conversation soon turned to Shaquille O'Neal, who at the time held Kareem's former position as the Lakers' starting center. He had been in the news for missing Chick's funeral, although he later announced he had been sick.

Shaq was also facing surgery on his arthritic right toe, to be performed at the Ronald Reagan UCLA Medical Center. Shaq's podiatrist was Dr. Robert Mohr, who is a close friend of mine.

After the Coach and I talked a little about Shaq's absence at Chick's funeral, our conversation shifted to the center's struggles at the free-throw line.

Coach Wooden was a terrific free-throw shooter during his playing days. Shaq, as we know, was not. I asked the Coach about Shaq's poor free-throw shooting.

"Shaq claims the ball is too small for his hands," he said. "That's hogwash; these players who have trouble with free-throw shooting just need to practice more."

How good was John Wooden at the free-throw line? Would you believe he once made 134 in a row in competition? That was when he was playing professionally in the 1930s. Professional basketball barely existed then, as there was no NBA, and thus no official records.

In the early 1970s, at one of Coach Wooden's camps at Cal Lutheran, he invited former Boston Celtic great Bill Sharman, then the coach of the Lakers, and Roger Staubach, who was on campus for the Dallas Cowboys training camp, to speak and join him in a free-throw exhibition.

Sharman was one of the best free-throw shooters in NBA history, and Coach Wooden said Staubach was also an excellent shooter.

A young camper asked Sharman how many free throws in a row he had made in competition. Sharman said he made 56 in a row twice, once during the regular season and once during the playoffs. The second streak of 56 came during 1958-59 playoffs. That is still the NBA playoff record.

The same camper then asked Wooden how many free throws in a row he had made in competition. Wooden said 134. It was when he was playing for a semi-pro team in Indianapolis known as the Kautskys. Their official name was the Kautsky Athletic Club.

The story goes that the owner of the team, Frank Kautsky, came out of the stands when the Coach's streak reached 100 and handed him a $100 bill as a bonus. The Coach was hesitant to take the money, but his wife Nell, who had also come out of the stands, grabbed the $100 bill. That was a lot of money in those days.

Years later, before his death in 2013, Sharman told the Los Angeles Times he was amazed when he heard the Coach say he had made 134 free throws in a row during competition. Who wouldn't be? It's as incredible as a golfer having a hole in one and a double eagle in the same round. But then Coach Wooden did that too.

He accomplished that feat in 1939 at the Erskine Park Golf Course in South Bend, Indiana. He aced the par-3, 149-yard sixth hole with a five iron and got a double-eagle 2 on the par-5 16th hole. His scorecard, signed by six people, shows he shot a four-over-par 75. According to Golf Digest, the Coach is one of only four people to have ever had a recorded hole-in-one and a double eagle in the same round.

The Coach was also a pool shark. There were stories where he would find a couple of his players shooting pool during a road trip and approach them with questions about what they were doing. When they got around to inviting him to pick up a cue, he often ran the table and walked off without saying a word.

One time he found two of his star players, Lew Alcindor and Lucius Allen, playing pool in their dorm. The Coach pointed out they should be studying rather than playing pool. They agreed, but first Allen, who had a reputation of being a pretty good pool hustler, challenged the Coach to a game. That was a mistake.

"When he missed, he never left the cue ball where I had a shot," Allen would say years later. "At the end, he winked and said, 'Now, Lucius, if I can beat you, you don't have much of a chance of making a living at this game. I suggest you go to the library.'"

Some of the tales of Coach's many athletic skills might be hard for future generations to believe. They might also question how one coach could win 10 national college basketball championships in a 12-year span, or have a team win 88 straight games. But we know that is true.

Remember, we're talking about an amazing man.

Chapter 4:
VIP Treatment at VIP's

I earlier mentioned VIP's, the coffee shop Coach frequented. He went there almost daily, with at least one or two guests. For me, going there with Coach was always a memorable event.

It was a place where, as the jingle from *Cheers* goes, "Everybody knows your name." Everybody knew Coach Wooden's name, and he knew the names of every employee, including the bus boys.

On our first visit, he rattled off the names of waiters Sandy, Bill, Jenny and Tom. This was my second visit to VIP's with the Coach, and both times we missed Tom. It was after 8:30 a.m., and the Coach explained Tom's graveyard shift had ended.

Yes, the Coach even knew the work shifts.

He always sat at table No. 2, a booth located in northeast corner of the restaurant. He ordered the No. 1 on the menu, which was two eggs, two pancakes, and two slices of bacon or sausage, or the No. 2, which was two eggs, two slices of bacon or sausage, and either toast or biscuit and gravy.

The waiters and busboys would all come over to say hello and he would shake the hands of each and every one of them and wish them a good day.

As I got to know the Coach, I became more and more aware of his warmth.

I noticed it every time he greeted me at his home, I noticed it when I would leave and he would give me a hug and say, "Give my best to your family and of course your father," and I would notice it in the way he treated others. There's an old saying that I find generally true: "Be wary of the person who is nice to you but rude to the waiter. He is not a nice person."

Judging from the way the Coach treated everyone at VIP's, he was a very nice person.

He was also a good conversationalist and willingly answered all my questions. During all of the time I spent with Coach throughout the years, I don't recall there ever being a lull in the conversation.

"Did you ever consider coaching in the NBA?" I asked him during one of our breakfasts at VIP's.

"No, but I did have a few opportunities," he said.

He said both the Lakers, when Jack Kent Cooke owned the team, and the Chicago Bulls made legitimate offers. And Irv Levin, who at one point owned the San Diego Clippers, made a particularly attractive offer to the Coach and his wife Nell.

In 1978, Levin and a partner bought the Boston Celtics and swapped them for the Buffalo Braves and moved the Braves to San Diego, where they were renamed the Clippers.

"He asked me where I wanted to live, and I told him Nell loved La Jolla," the Coach said. "He was going to build us a home there, and I almost accepted his offer, but I didn't want to be away from the rest of my family."

Levin sold the Clippers to Donald Sterling in 1981, and Sterling moved the team to Los Angeles in 1984. Today Steve Ballmer owns the Clippers and I am the team's podiatrist.

Speaking of coaching positions, it has been well documented that the Coach almost ended up at the University of Minnesota instead of UCLA in 1948. He would have accepted Minnesota's offer had he initially been allowed to bring Ed Powell, his assistant at Indiana State, with him. That was a sticking point.

UCLA was also after the Coach and agreed to let him bring Powell with him.

The Minnesota athletic director finally agreed to go along with the Coach's request and attempted to call to let him know. But a snowstorm either delayed the call or temporarily knocked out phone service. It has been reported both ways.

By the time the Minnesota athletic director got through to the Coach, UCLA Athletic Director Wilbur Johns, who had also been serving as the basketball coach, had already reached Coach Wooden on the phone.

The Coach accepted Johns' offer. When the Minnesota athletic director called later the same day, Coach Wooden faced a difficult decision. As it turned out, he didn't want to go back on his word to UCLA and felt that since he had accepted the coaching position with the school out west, he must honor that.

UCLA gave the Coach a three-year contract. After two seasons, when the Bruins went 22-7 and 24-7, an offer came from Purdue University. The school in West Layette, Indiana, gave the Coach the opportunity to return home to the Midwest as the Boilermakers' head coach.

"I wanted to take that job and return to the state of Indiana," he told me during our initial breakfast at VIP's. "But I felt I needed to fulfill my contract with UCLA before making a change. If I had signed only for two years, I probably would have gone."

The next year, after UCLA had a record of 19-10, Purdue was no longer looking for a new head coach. Since there were no other possibilities that interested Coach, he stayed at UCLA, signing one-year contracts throughout the rest of his career at the university.

Eventually it became time to leave VIP's. The Coach would be back the next day, when his breakfast guests would be former players Kenny Heitz and Andy Hill. A few days after that, former player Kenny Washington would dine with him.

As he and I left the restaurant, the Coach said goodbye to all the employees. He found the sports section of a newspaper on top of the trash, picked it up and put it under his arm.

"I'll read this when I get home," he told me.

We walked to my car at a slow pace due to his arthritis. After he had gingerly gotten into my car, I asked the Coach if he still drove. He said he did. He owned a 1989 Ford Taurus with 32,000 miles on it. At this point in his life, he was still driving it around town.

I learned later he never gave up his passion for that car. It was still parked in the garage at his condominium building when he died in 2010. By then it had about 40,000 miles on the odometer. He still had a driver's license at age 99, although he hadn't been physically able to drive for years.

Chapter 5:
Recruiting Philosophies

We touched on many topics during my early sessions with the Coach at his home. Our conversations often took place in his den, where the phone rang constantly. He screened most of the calls, picking up only after they had gone to his answering machine.

The message on the answering machine would say, "Please speak slowly and distinctly and leave your name after the tone." You could tell his background included being a high school English teacher.

He usually only picked up when he recognized the voice or name, but sometimes he picked up regardless. Amazingly, his phone number was listed in the white pages.

I recall one fellow from Arizona kept calling. Finally, the Coach picked up. The voice on the other end rambled on and on. Among other things, the man said he wanted to give the Coach $100,000. It was people like this that made him screen his calls.

One topic we discussed that I found particularly interesting was recruiting. He told me he rarely visited a recruit. For the most part, he left that to his assistants. He also almost never left the state of California for recruits, believing it had more talent than any other state in the country.

He did, however, fly to New York in 1964 to visit the father of a recruit, Ferdinand Lewis Alcindor Sr. Lew Alcindor's father worked the night shift as a transit police officer, and his mother was a price checker at a department store. His son Lew, who later became Kareem Abdul-Jabbar, had already committed to UCLA, and the Coach wanted to ensure the Alcindors that he would take good care of their son.

A special relationship with Lew Alcindor/Kareem Abdul-Jabbar that began in 1964 continued on through the rest of Coach's life.

The Coach, accompanied by assistant coach Jerry Norman, took a late flight to New York and met with Mr. Alcindor when he got off work around 2 a.m. and then headed to the airport to catch an early flight to Kansas City. Norman had convinced the Coach that on the way back to Los Angeles they should stop off in Kansas City to visit with another prize recruit, Lucius Allen, and his mother.

Allen had been also considering going to the University of Colorado before the visit from the Coach and Norman. That trip to K.C. accomplished two things. It locked up Allen, a future All-American, and helped convince Alcindor he had made a good choice in picking UCLA.

Many years later, Kareem became one of my patients, as well as a friend. I assist him with some of his charitable work, including the Skyhook Foundation's summer camp, a five-day educational adventure for fourth and fifth graders. It is held in collaboration with the Los Angeles Unified School District. The camp's site is located in the Angeles National Forest, about an hour's drive northeast from Los Angeles.

I have found Kareem to be a most interesting man, as attested by the excellent 2015 HBO documentary, "Kareem: Minority of One."

In the film, Kareem says he was impressed with the palm trees and grass when he first visited UCLA, and that he received a letter from UCLA alum Jackie Robinson.

"Coach Wooden made it very clear he wanted me to stay at UCLA for four years and get my degree, and that's what I wanted too," Kareem says in the film.

In my conversations with Kareem, his fondness for Coach Wooden comes through loud and clear. He was impressed with Coach Wooden after their first meeting, saying: "I appreciated the way he carried himself, and the total lack or pretense and arrogance. Other coaches, like [Kentucky's] Adolph Rupp, were very high profile, flamboyant. They didn't have the appeal to me that John Wooden did."

Of course it proved worthwhile for the Coach to leave California to recruit Lew Alcindor. A few years later, he chose not to visit with another prized east coast recruit, John Shumate of Elizabeth, New Jersey, and he ended up regretting that decision.

Nan Wooden said she was attending a UCLA game against Gonzaga at Pauley Pavilion in December of 2014 when, after entering the arena well before game time, a tall middle-aged black man stopped her.

"You're Coach Wooden's daughter, aren't you?" the man said. "My name is John Shumate, and I've got a story to tell you."

"I'd like to hear it," Nan told him.

"In 1970, I was the No. 1 high school recruit on the East Coast," Shumate said, "and I wanted to play for your dad at UCLA. He sent Denny Crum to scout me at one of my games.

"Unfortunately, during that game one of my teammates got in a fight with an opposing player. I went over to help break up the fight and things got a little out of hand. From what I understand, Coach Crum told your dad that I wasn't the type of player they wanted at UCLA.

"Years later at a Final Four, I can't remember the exact year, I talked with your dad and he told me that one of his biggest regrets was not recruiting me himself.

"I just thought you'd want to know that."

Nan said she thanked him for telling her that story.

Instead of going to UCLA, Shumate ended up going to Notre Dame, where he was a freshman when the team beat UCLA, 89-82, on January 23, 1971. The Bruins didn't lose another game until they lost to Notre Dame on January 19, 1974. In between was their amazing 88-game win streak.

In 1974, Shumate, a senior, was the starting center for Notre Dame. He scored 24 points in the 71-70 victory. When the game ended, it was Shumate who threw the ball high in the air as the final seconds ticked off.

Shumate would years later tell *The New York Times* that he prayed with his parents over the phone the night before that 1974 game.

After playing in the NBA for six seasons, he got into coaching. He was the head coach at Southern Methodist University (SMU) for seven seasons and later the head coach of the Phoenix Mercury of the WNBA. He has been an assistant coach for several NBA teams.

Apparently, he was Wooden's type of player after all.

Nan Wooden and John Shumate at Pauley Pavilion in 2014.

There were certain kinds of players the Coach stayed clear of, such as those with poor grades. The Coach said the first thing he evaluated about a recruit was academic performance. If a player did not have good grades, he was not interested in him.

He usually had only six or seven players each year that he really wanted and would end up with two or three of them.

He would have his assistant coach call the parents of a recruit and ask them to send their son's high school transcripts.

If there were certain subjects where a recruit struggled in school, the Coach would make sure that he was tutored in those subjects. And he would follow through to make sure there was no slacking off down the road.

He believed in a low-key approach to recruiting. He said he wanted players who wanted to play at UCLA. He didn't want to have to talk them into it. He said he rarely did home visits.

"I believe I visited the homes of maybe a dozen prospects in my 27 years at UCLA," he said. "Visiting homes is too high pressured."

He told me that, instead, he liked for recruits to visit the campus, where they were able to talk to his players.

When he had a prospect in mind, the first thing he wanted to find out was his grades. The next step was to see how quick this player was in relation to other players at that positon.

Another important aspect in choosing a prospect, he said, was if he was a team player or perhaps he could be taught to be one.

Coach Wooden knew the importance of recruiting. He always said, "You can't go to war without a soldier."

Chapter 6:
Love and Poetry

It had been several months since I had made a house call for the Coach. I was particularly looking forward to this visit, which was scheduled for a Saturday. Sometimes I would see the Coach on a weekend, which gave me more time with him.

I had missed him—not only his interesting topics of conversations, but also his warmth. There were the usual warm greetings at the elevator after he had buzzed me in. Then there were the hugs when we said goodbye.

And he always asked, "How is your dad? Tell him hello for me."

It was like visiting your favorite uncle. Only in this case, the uncle was a legendary person.

On this visit, I brought along my cousin, Brad Kaplan. I think Brad was a little nervous about meeting an icon, but the Coach immediately made him feel at ease. Coach Wooden had that ability to make people feel comfortable within minutes. Many of my friends would remark that they felt as if they had known Coach for years after only a half hour with him.

After we got settled in, I treated the Coach's feet. When we finished and went back to the living room, Brad asked him if he ever had a losing season as a competitor and a coach. He said he might have had one, his first year coaching high school, or maybe two. We know he never had a losing season in his 27 years at UCLA or in his two at Indiana State.

Brad asked, "What is your secret to winning?"

"It's very simple," the Coach said. "The word is love."

That was the Coach's favorite word. He loved his wife, he loved his family, and he loved people. He particularly loved his players.

"Some needed more love than others," he said. "Some needed a pat on the back while others needed a kick in the behind."

One player he spoke fondly of on this day was Swen Nater, the 6-foot-11 backup center to Bill Walton for two seasons. Nater, a native of the Netherlands, had come from Cypress College with a lot of raw ability.

Swen Nater

Nater never started a college game but was a first-round pick in both the ABA and NBA drafts in 1973. He was the ABA's rookie of the year while playing for the San Antonio Spurs, then an ABA team. The following season, he led the league in rebounding with the San Diego Clippers. After the ABA-NBA merger in 1976, Nater led the NBA in rebounding with the San Diego Clippers in the 1979-80 season, making him the only player to ever lead both leagues in rebounding.

It wasn't only Nater's playing ability that made him a favorite of the Coach; it was also their common interest in poetry.

The Coach often entertained guests by reading poetry, as he did on this day. He went to his cabinet and pulled out a manila folder filled with Nater's poems and began reading. Many of Nater's poems were about the Coach, but modesty keeps him from reading those. A book of Nater's poems, *A Reason for the Rhyme*, dedicated to the Coach, was published in 2006. Here is a poem from that book:

I STILL PUT MY SOCKS ON
THE VERY SAME WAY

It has been many years since I was a collegian
But I still can remember that very first day
When my teacher bent down with a sock demonstration
And I still put my socks on the very same way.

Now I'm fifty and one and he's over ninety
And now both of us glitter with silver and gray
And I don't play much hoops now, nor tennis or handball
But I still put my socks on the very same way.

My teacher lives far from the place that I live now.
When I pull up my socks, I can still hear him say,
"You must start with the toes and smooth over the ankles."
So I still put my socks on the very same way.

Oh don't get me wrong now, there have been temptations
Just to leave a small wrinkle and sin for a day,
And to take a small chance of just one little blister.
But I still put my socks on the very same way.

So what's so important 'bout proper sock fitting
And what does "no wrinkles" have to do with today?
It's a pound of the cure but an ounce of prevention.
So I still put my socks on the very same way.

So I still love the game and I still love the contest
And I still love the mem'ries of when we would play.
Yes, I still love my coach and I still love my teacher
And I still put my socks on the very same way.

Coach Wooden is shown in his study as he
reads one of Swen Nater's poems.

The Coach's fondness for poetry dates to his high school days in Martinsville, Indiana. His high school sweetheart, and eventually his wife of 53 years, Nell, persuaded him to take a speech class to help him get out of his shell. Young John Wooden was very shy and struggled when reading aloud in the class until the teacher had him read a poem. Reading poetry made speaking easier.

Besides poetry, the Coach also loved baseball. That was also a topic of discussion on the day my cousin and I were at his home. "Baseball was my first love, and it is my favorite sport," he told us.

He excelled in both baseball and basketball as a youngster, and he lettered in track for two years at Martinsville High, finishing sixth in the state in the 100-yard dash as a senior. He might have pursued baseball over basketball in high school, but Martinsville did not field a baseball team. He had to look elsewhere to play organized baseball. He usually played shortstop.

The summer after high school, he was playing a game in Indianapolis. When at the plate, he turned into a fastball and got hit in the shoulder.

"I went from having a great arm to no arm at all," he said. "That ended my baseball playing career."

But it didn't end his love for baseball.

Of the literally millions of newspaper articles written about John Wooden, there was only one clipping he kept folded up in his wallet. It was a short item from *The Pittsburgh Press*. It was about an offer from the Pittsburgh Pirates in 1963 for the Coach to become the team's manager.

The back-story is that Joe Brown, general manager of the Pirates and son of the great Hollywood comedic actor Joe E. Brown, was in Los Angeles for a dinner and was seated next to John Wooden. Brown and the Coach talked baseball throughout the evening, and Brown was so enraptured with the Coach's baseball knowledge that he later called him from Pittsburgh and offered him the managerial job.

Coach Wooden said he told Brown, "If I take you up on this, who do you think they'd fire first, you or me? If I were the owner, I'd fire you first for hiring me. Then I'd fire me."

He then added, "It was ridiculous, absolutely ridiculous. But I still keep the clipping just for fun."

Brad and I enjoyed seeing the clipping and hearing the story behind it. It was part of a very pleasant visit that lasted a couple of hours. As we left, the Coach hugged me and shook hands with Brad.

I appreciated the Coach's hugs over the years, particularly since I don't think he was overly demonstrative in expressing affection. But there was a gentle demeanor that conveyed his kindness and warmth.

Again, I saw a similarity between my father and the Coach in this regard. My dad also used gentleness and kindness to convey affection.

Chapter 7:

Always Seeing the Best in People

In my visits with the Coach at his home, he would talk fondly about his players. He never directed any harsh criticism at any of them, at least not to me.

One prominent player he could have legitimately criticized was Lucius Allen. He had become an All-American guard on the 1967 and 1968 national championship teams, but he missed his senior season (also Lew Alcindor's senior season) after receiving a second citation for marijuana possession.

Allen was again cited for marijuana possession in 1972 in Milwaukee while playing for the Bucks, and rumors of drug use haunted him for years.

When Allen's name came up during one of our early conversations, the Coach acknowledged he had "gone through some hard times." The Coach knew about the drug rumors and that his first wife had committed suicide. According to newspaper reports, Melanie Rose Allen died of carbon monoxide intoxication at the age of 34 in 1982. Lucius discovered the body in the back seat of their car in the garage of their home in suburban Kansas City.

"Lucius' life is improving," the Coach told me. "He has remarried and appears to be happy."

The Coach said he remained friends with many of his former players and kept track of them. He was proud of the fact that so many have been successful in life.

"Almost all my players graduated," he enjoyed saying. "Most of them have gone on to great success. I've got doctors, lawyers, teachers, and eight ministers."

Many players phoned the Coach regularly, particularly Nater and Bill Walton. He said Walton was the most frequent caller.

"He called me 24 times from the Sydney Olympics," the Coach said during one of my visits in 2002, two years after those Games.

One time when I was at the Coach's home, the phone rang and as usual he let the answering machine pick up the call. It was Walton's booming voice, and the Coach said to me, "It's Bill, so don't pick up the phone. If you do, I'll be on for an hour."

Then we heard, "Coach, Bill Walton here. It's a beautiful afternoon in sunny San Diego and I'm riding my new bike. The sky is blue, the ocean is clear, and there is no one else I'd rather share this moment with than you, Coach. Just thought I'd let you know I'm thinking of you. I love you." And he hung up.

The Coach loved Walton as a player. He would rave about how hard he worked in practice, about his quick and proper execution of fundamentals, his boyish enthusiasm for the game, and his consideration for his teammates, which made him such an unselfish player.

As for Walton as a person, that was a love affair that grew over time.

Walton was not always the easiest person to deal with off the court.

Wooden has been quoted as saying, "There's an age when we all test people in authority. Bill tended to question many things, and sometimes not with the most tact."

One day Walton came into the Coach's office and said he wanted to try marijuana as a pain reliever.

"Bill, I haven't heard that it is a pain reliever, but I have heard that it is illegal," the Coach told him.

Walton was generally viewed as anti-establishment, someone who was quick to get involved with protests against the Vietnam War and other civil causes. He was a rebel with a cause in those days, and viewed as a member of the hippie generation.

"He would hitchhike all around, and I would be concerned that he might not come back to school," the Coach told me. "But he always did."

The Coach also talked about the time when Walton was a senior and came to practice unshaven and with hair covering his ears. This is an often-told story, and here is my version, as told to me by the Coach.

"We had a 10-day break—no practices and no games," he began, "when Bill showed up at practice with a beard and long hair. I gave him a look, and he knew what was coming next.

"He starts in, 'I'm a two-time college player of the year, we've won two national championships, we haven't lost a game since I've been on the varsity, I'm an Academic All-American, I'm going to graduate in three and a half years . . .'

"He continues on, saying, 'I don't think you have the right to tell me how long my hair should be or if I can have facial hair or not.'"

"I said, 'Bill, you are correct. I do not have the right to tell you that, but I do have the right to decide if you will continue to be a member of this team. We've enjoyed your time here and we're going to miss you.'"

Walton, who enjoys telling this story as well, has often said he immediately went and jumped on his bicycle, rode as quickly as he could to a Westwood barber shop and said, "Cut it off, cut it all off."

After that, anytime the Coach and Walton had a disagreement, all the Coach had to say was, "Bill, we're going to miss you." That would be the end of it.

A major turning point in Walton's life took place in 1981, when he was 28. Like the Coach at a young age, Walton had trouble speaking in front of groups. Only for Walton, it was more serious, and he also had a bad stuttering problem. Neither poetry reading nor anything else helped.

Dr. Ernie Vandeweghe, a former New York Knicks player and the father of former Bruin Kiki Vandeweghe, told Walton he knew a man in New York who might be able to help him.

That man was Marty Glickman, an Olympic sprinter who became a prominent New York radio play-by-play announcer. At one time or other, he did games for the Knicks, Jets, and Giants. He later also became a voice coach for announcers at NBC Sports.

Dr. Vandeweghe arranged for Glickman to come to San Diego to meet Walton. They spent most of a weekend on a boat in Mission Bay, a peaceful setting where Glickman showed Walton exercises that would help him.

Years later, Walton told a *Los Angeles Times* reporter that his session with Glickman had changed his life.

When contacted by that reporter, Glickman was a bit taken aback. "I knew we got some things accomplished," he said, "but I had no idea Bill is giving me all the credit. He did most of it himself."

Walton captured my feelings about Coach with this quote, which also appeared in the Times: "People who don't know John Wooden come up to me and say, 'Ah, come on, you talk like he's perfect.' I tell them that he isn't perfect. That actually he's better than that."

I was fortunate to get to know Bill Walton through Coach Wooden. We presented Bill with the Loyola Lions shirt he is wearing here when he was a guest speaker at my class at Loyola Marymount University.

Chapter 8:
The Coach and His Neighbor

During my next visit to his condo, I wanted to talk about his love for baseball. I asked, "Coach, are you a Dodgers fan?"

"Very much so," he said.

Here's a story not too many people know about.

In the spring of 1958, Coach and Nell were living in an apartment complex in Brentwood that had a wrought-iron fence protecting it.

One day Coach was coming home and he noticed a distinguished-looking man with red hair at the gate balancing two bags of groceries while trying to open the gate to the complex.

He came to the man's rescue and opened the gate. The Coach then volunteered to carry one of the bags of groceries. The man said thank you and he invited the Coach to come inside his apartment so they could visit.

The man explained he was new to the area, having just moved into the complex. He said he had been living in the New York area and working in Brooklyn.

The Coach asked him what brought him out west, and the man said, "I'm an announcer for the Dodgers, who as you probably know have moved here. My name is Vin Scully."

Wooden then introduced himself, explaining he coached basketball over at a nearby college, UCLA.

They were no doubt aware of each other, but in those days few sports events were televised and announcers for the most part were heard, not seen, so neither man recognized the other.

Scully explained to his new friend and neighbor that he had visited the Los Angeles area only once before, during a brief stint in the Navy toward the tail end of World War II. He had befriended a fellow sailor whose parents lived in Brentwood, and when their ship docked in Los Angeles, the friend took young Vin Scully with him to visit his parents.

When Walter O'Malley, the owner of the Dodgers, asked Scully in 1958 where he wanted to live when the team moves to Los Angeles, Scully mentioned the only area he knew, Brentwood.

His chance meeting with Coach was the start of a long friendship—and a mutual admiration—between two of Southern California's greatest sports legends.

"He didn't live in our complex for very long," Wooden said of his former neighbor. "He and his wife moved to a larger, nicer place. I believe it was in Pacific Palisades. But we remained friends."

Of Scully as an announcer, the Coach said: "Vin is absolutely, unquestionably the greatest sports announcer of all time. He's remarkable. He can do any sport, but in baseball, no one's close."

Here's another amazing small-world story, told to me by his daughter Nan.

When the Coach and Nell arrived in Southern California in 1948, they needed to find a church near Brentwood. They found a list of churches in the area and noticed that the minister at the First Christian Church of Santa Monica was named Wales Smith.

They wondered if it could be the same Wales Smith they knew as the minister at the First Christian Church of Martinsville, Indiana. Nell told the Coach, "It has to be. Smith is a common name, but Wales certainly isn't."

It was the same man Nell had known since she was a small child, having attended his church. And that is how they found their church in this new place out west.

It's well known that Wooden was a religious man who attended church every Sunday, when possible. He was a church deacon in both Martinsville and Santa Monica. There was one thing he told me about the First Christian Church of Santa Monica that I found particularly interesting.

The Coach was generally viewed as prim and proper, someone who would always wear a coat and tie to church. In the old days, a coat, tie and slacks were sometimes called your "Sunday-go-to-meeting" clothes. But things changed over the years, and the Coach told me he liked the fact a coat and tie were no longer required at his church.

"You don't need to get dressed up," he said. "You can even wear shorts if you like."

Here's yet another small-world story. When Coach and Nell arrived in Southern California, they were also looking for a doctor in the area when they saw the name Dr. Ralph Irwin in a phone book. It turned out this was the same doctor who performed an emergency appendectomy years earlier on the Coach when he was in Navy and stationed in Iowa City, not long after the start of World War II. The Coach and Nell had grown fond of Dr. Irwin, so he was an obvious choice as their doctor, just as Wales Smith had been an obvious choice as their minister.

And there is another twist to this story. The appendicitis kept the Coach from reporting for duty as a fitness office aboard the USS *Franklin*, an aircraft carrier stationed in the South Pacific.

The man who went in Coach Wooden's place was a friend from Purdue. Several months later, he and dozens of other men were killed when a Japanese kamikaze pilot struck the ship.

Had the Coach been on board, he likely would have been killed.

Chapter 9:
A Daughter's Special Day

I spoke with Coach by phone during baseball season and invited him to attend a Dodgers game with me. It was a day game because I knew the Coach only liked to go to day games.

He had told me several weeks earlier that he would be interested in going to a game. I was pretty sure he would be, since baseball was always his favorite sport. But when I called him with my invitation, he declined. He said he would like to go but he would need a cart to get around, and that would be an embarrassment. He explained he could no longer walk long distances. He was 92 at the time.

I was disappointed but tried not to show it. I told the Coach I would see him at his home in a couple of days.

It was three days later when I made my next house call. I spent an afternoon at his home, and this time I brought along my daughter Rachel. She was 11 at the time.

On this occasion, the Coach's son-in-law, Dick Muelhausen, Nan's husband, was there. He had requested that I examine his feet, which I did after we talked for a bit. Dick suffered from diabetes. He was also on dialysis, and had undergone quadruple heart bypass surgery. Dick passed way in 2004, and I was glad I had a chance to meet him.

We talked about the Coach's schedule and how full it was. He had given one of his inspirational lectures the day before, and on the upcoming weekend he was scheduled for a four-hour autograph session at the annual Los Angeles Times/UCLA Book Fair.

On this day, I found the Coach to be a little under the weather. He had a cold and was taking antibiotics. He felt his speech the day before didn't go very well because of his cold.

Dick explained that Coach's schedule included 30 speeches a year for American Agencies, a statewide mutual fund company with offices in Torrance, Anaheim, San Diego, and San Francisco.

Dick said he attended many of Wooden's talks. He said each talk was different. He said he always learned something new at each one. He added that the Coach tailored his speeches to fit the audience he was addressing.

Dick said Coach rarely said no to anybody, and at times it was simply too much. He and Nan were always trying to get him to cut back.

Dick explained that the money the Coach made from public appearances went into a trust for his 13 great grandchildren, including one with special needs, Cameron Trapani.

Cameron had a stroke in the womb about five months into his mother Kathleen's pregnancy. Doctors didn't think he would live. He had heart surgery at age one and a half, and his disabilities remain severe. His mother, with help from family and friends, cared for him for 20 years before he was moved to a highly respected special facility in Chatsworth, California. He now lives in a facility in Chatsworth.

Cameron's brother, Tyler Trapani, made news on February 26, 2011. As a walk-on reserve on the UCLA basketball team who rarely played, he made the final shot on the old Nell and John

Wooden Court at Pauley Pavilion before the arena was totally remodeled. It didn't reopen until 2013.

Tyler Trapani and his grandmother, Nan Wooden, are shown at a 2015 luncheon with co-author Larry Stewart and his wife Norma.

As my conversation with Dick Muelhausen continued, I told him about the Coach declining my invitation to go to a Dodgers game.

"He really does feel embarrassed about being in a large crowd and needing extra help getting around," Dick said.

Dick said he was actually surprised that his father-in-law accepted the offer to throw out the first pitch at a World Series game the previous year at Angel Stadium.

"He did admit afterwards that he enjoyed doing it," Dick added.

On this day, what I enjoyed most was having my daughter meet Coach.

As I treated Dick, Rachel and Coach were able to spend 15 to 20 minutes together in the study. He read poetry to her, showed her pictures of his grandchildren and great grandchildren, and told her about some of the many trophies in his trophy case. Coach also went over each of the blocks in his Pyramid of Success. He told her that success is not always measured by A's and B's in school. He said as long as you try to do your best, that is what is most important.

"Doing your best is a sign of success," he said.

He then recited a quotation to Rachel. It went something like this:

> At God's footstool to confess
> A poor soul knelt and bowed his head
> I failed he cried
> The master said
> Thou did thy best, and that is success.

When it came time for me to treat Coach's feet, he seemed as happy and as lucid as ever. However, his voice was somewhat nasal and raspy because of the cold.

He was concerned about the swelling in his ankles, which were larger than usual. I understood his concern but felt confident the swelling would go down.

Earlier, I had mentioned that I was going to Indianapolis and planned to visit his hometown of Martinsville. The trip was now only two weeks away. I think he had forgotten about my plans, but he smiled when I reminded him. He told me some of the places to go in Martinsville, and specifically mentioned the Candy Kitchen on Main Street. He asked me to bring back some candy for him.

After I was done with his treatment, my daughter and I sat with Coach in his study.

Coach told us he had written several children's books. With Coach, nothing much surprised me anymore. This was another way to introduce the Pyramid of Success to young people, in this case very young people. Coach worked on the project with authors Steve Jamison, Bonnie Graves and Peanut Louie Harper. The illustrator was Susan F. Cornelison.

Coach also recited more poetry for us from memory. I was always amazed by his memory. This man remembered all his players from his teams in the 20's and their starting positions. When old friends came by to visit, he remembered such detail that even his friends were astonished with his memory. There is an old Chinese proverb, "The larger the ears, the better the memory." Well, my friend did have large ears, and an incredible memory.

Then we talked about a benefit I was involved with that was coming up in October. It was for Upward Bound House, a Santa Monica nonprofit that provides temporary housing to homeless families. The event was a dinner at the Skirball Cultural Center.

I had asked the Coach to come, and he said he would and was looking forward to it. I also asked if he could arrange for a few of his former players to attend as well, and he said he would do that. He was able to get us Walton and Keith Erickson.

This photo of me and my wife Lori was taken at the Upward Bound House fundraiser.

As we were talking about the event, another former player, Andy Hill, came to the door. Andy was a reserve on three of Coach Wooden's championship teams (1970-72) and had gone on to a successful career in television and entertainment. At one point, he was a top executive at CBS, heading up the network's production department.

Hill had written a fascinating book about his relationship with the Coach, published in 2001 and titled *Be Quick – But Don't Hurry: Finding Success in the Teachings of a Lifetime.*

I found Andy to be cordial and polite. I invited him to our charity dinner in October, and he said he would love to come. Andy had just come back from Texas, where he had delivered a lecture about his book and his relationship with the Coach.

The phone rang several times during our conversations that afternoon. The Coach said he was expecting a phone call from Walton, whom he hadn't heard from in several days. I think the Coach was concerned. It was unlike Walton not to call.

All in all it had been a good day. The Coach seemed in good spirits, despite his cold, and once again I hugged him goodbye.

He didn't want to hug my daughter because he didn't want to give her his cold. Rachel was gracious and excited as she said goodbye, and it was clear that she had enjoyed this special visit.

Chapter 10:
My Visit to Martinsville

Finally, I took my much-anticipated trip to Indiana. I spent a couple of days in Indianapolis visiting my friend Michael Helms from podiatry school and seeing some of the sights.

Two days later, I made the one-hour drive southwest to Martinsville, which is considered John Robert Wooden's hometown. Coach spent the first four years of his life there and then returned prior to the sophomore year of high school. His parents remained there the rest of their lives.

In 1914, the Coach's family moved away from Martinsville to two other small communities in the area, first Hall and then Monrovia, before settling on a 60-acre farm outside Centerton in 1915. The farm, which had been owned by Coach's mother's family, consisted of wheat, corn, alfalfa, potatoes, watermelons, tomatoes and timothy grass, which was used to feed cattle and horses.

In 1925, due to financial hardships, the farm was lost and the Wooden family, which then consisted of parents Hugh and Roxie and their four boys, moved back to Martinsville. Roxie earlier gave birth to two girls, but one died of diphtheria at age three, and three and a half months later another died during delivery.

The move back to Martinsville exposed the Wooden boys to basketball. Indiana is known for its passion for basketball, and the people in Martinsville exemplified that passion.

The Martinsville High School gymnasium, a massive redbrick edifice opened in 1924, was built to Hoosier Hysteria scale. The original capacity was 5,200—in a town with a population of 4,800 at the time.

In January 1989, it became the John R. Wooden Gymnasium. The Coach, along with many dignitaries and celebrities, came to Martinsville for the renaming ceremony. The Coach's signature is on the court, and the trophy case contains pictures of a teenage Wooden in uniform. A huge high-top sneaker in the school lobby is decorated on one side with the coach's famed Pyramid of Success. Near the school is a street that bears the name John R. Wooden Drive.

The Coach visited Martinsville whenever he was in the area, which was often after the establishment in 1994 of the John R. Wooden Tradition in Indianapolis, an annual basketball double-header. Whenever he drove down to Martinsville, he always made a point of stopping at the small cemetery in Centerton, seven miles from Martinsville, where his parents and two sisters are buried.

From 1926-28, Martinsville High went to three straight state championship games, losing when John Bob, as Coach was sometimes called, was a sophomore and a senior and winning his junior year. When Martinsville won the state title, John Wooden was the team's leading scorer with 10 points in a 26-23 victory over Muncie Central in the championship game. The tournament began with 731 teams.

Years later, in visits to Martinsville, Coach often told the townspeople that winning that state title his junior year was the highlight of his entire career in basketball—and that is saying something.

Martinsville and Muncie Central met again in the state championship game the following year, when Wooden was a senior, and this time Muncie Central won 13-12. The winning basket was a half-court fling at the basket. "It was the highest-arching shot I ever saw," the Coach said in recalling that game.

Martinsville High is also where the Coach, during his sophomore year, met a cute freshman with an upturned pixie nose named Nellie Riley. They soon became inseparable, and were married in 1932. It was the first and only person the Coach ever dated.

During one of my earlier visits to his home, the Coach had talked with me about his childhood. He said he wasn't rich in a monetary way, but he was rich in other ways and had the love and guidance of both parents. Despite considerable misfortune, his father never complained.

As I drove to Martinsville, I thought about all I had read and heard about John Wooden's hometown. The drive was a peaceful one. Churches dotted the area, and there were small rivers everywhere.

I finally saw a sign that said Martinsville. I turned off Highway 37 and slowly drove into the sleepy little town that reminded me of Mayberry, the fictional home of Sheriff Andy Taylor, Opie, Aunt Bee, and Deputy Barney Fife.

But this was real life, and for me it was very emotional. I had been thinking about my visit for months, and now I was here. While driving through town, I came across Main Street. I got out of my car and walked around.

The streets were somewhat bare on this Saturday afternoon. I spotted the candy store that Coach Wooden had mentioned to me and hustled on over.

When I walked into Martinsville Candy Kitchen, it was pretty much as I had envisioned it. It was an old-fashioned candy store with a soda fountain and ice cream parlor. The store featured handmade candy canes, divinity, peanut-butter fudge, cinnamon logs, English toffees and many other delicacies.

An older lady greeted me. I asked her what was the candy of the day, and she replied that everybody liked the peanut-butter fudge. I ordered a half-pound for the Coach and sealed it up.

I was then off to see the rest of the town. I found John R. Wooden Drive and also got to see Martinsville High. Before my visit to Martinsville ended, a quiet eerie feeling came over me. I knew the Ku Klux Klan had been a major presence in Martinsville and throughout much of Indiana in the 1920s. I also knew racism was something the Coach had fought against his entire life.

I sort of smiled to myself and shivered a bit at the same time as I thought about what the reaction would have been to a Jewish man such as myself visiting this town during the days when the KKK was so prevalent.

More importantly, I got a firsthand look at the roots of John Robert Wooden. That's what I came to see.

As I drove out of town toward Indianapolis, I stopped to visit the cemetery in nearby Centerton, where his parents are laid to rest. Then it was time to drive back to Indianapolis and catch a plane home.

Chapter 11:

Delivering Candy and Meeting Jim Wooden

It was about two weeks after I returned from my trip to Indiana that I made my next visit to Coach's condominium. A pleasant surprise was that his son Jim was there. He had spent the night.

I was there to bring over the peanut-butter fudge candy I had brought from Martinsville. After exchanging pleasantries with Jim, I gave Coach the candy I had brought from the Martinsville Candy Kitchen. He thanked me profusely.

I also told him about the store clerk who had been excited when I told her I knew him. She asked me to tell him how much she appreciated it when the Coach mentioned the Martinsville Candy Kitchen on national television two years earlier.

I didn't want to leave Jim out of the conversation, so I directed some questions his way. He told me about joining the Marine Corps out of high school and about his career in sales. For many years he had worked for a welding supply company and also had sales jobs for similar companies. He said he enjoyed sales and the connection with people.

I found him to be gracious, much like his father, and he seemed relaxed throughout our conversation. Jim talked about his many visits to Martinsville with his father over the years. He and his sister and other family members accompanied the Coach to Indiana whenever he went back for the John R. Wooden Tradition in Indianapolis. The group would almost always take the opportunity to make the short trip to Martinsville.

When Jim Wooden was born in 1936, his father was coaching at South Bend Central High. In 1941, his father enlisted in the Navy and went to officer's training school.

Jim and his older sister Nan moved west with their parents when Jim was 12. Their first home had a basket hoop in the back yard, and Jim shot lots of hoops.

He said he was a decent player at University High, but he didn't have the skill level—or the grades—to play for UCLA. So he joined the Marine Corps. "Naturally, I am very proud of my dad and even more proud of him as a man than a coach," Jim said. "Many times when people would connect the two of us and discover I was his son, they would ask, 'Why aren't you coaching?' My reply would be, 'Well, my dad's dad was a farmer, but my dad didn't become a farmer.'"

After Jim left the Coach's home, I stuck around and the Coach and I talked more about Martinsville.

He said that although his family didn't have a lot of money he had a normal childhood.

When the Wooden family lost the farm in Centerton and moved back to Martinsville in 1925, the town was prospering due to artesian wells in the area. In fact, Martinsville High's nickname is the Artesians.

Nearly a dozen sanitariums were built in and around Martinsville. Hugh Wooden got a job as a masseur at the Home Lawn Sanitarium, the area's largest and most opulent resort. A big part of Hugh's income came from tips.

"I think that is why Daddy was always such a generous tipper," Nan Wooden told me.

I have a story to tell about Coach and tipping. When he was 98, he and Nan went out to dinner at a nice San Fernando Valley restaurant with a friend of mine and his wife. My friend and his wife had picked up the Coach and Nan at the Encino condo.

At the end of the evening, when my friend was getting his car from the parking valet, he asked his wife for a dollar to add to the tip. As the Coach was being helped into the front seat of my friend's car, he stopped everything, reached into his pocket and pulled out a wad of one-dollar bills. He peeled off one and handed it to my friend's wife.

"A lady should never have to pay," said the Coach, always a gentleman.

My friend's wife later asked Nan why her father carried all those one-dollar bills.

"That's his tip money," Nan said.

But back to my visit to Coach's home following my trip to Indiana. As we talked, the phone rang several times. The phone ringing at the Wooden's home was commonplace. On this day, one of the calls was from an assistant women's basketball coach at UC Santa Barbara. She had come to visit the Coach and she was downstairs.

The Coach told me that he had forgotten that she was coming, but I assured him that I had to be leaving anyway. Since we had already discussed his health issues and he was doing fine, I told him I was going back to my office.

Before I said goodbye, he apologized for forgetting about the visit from the women's basketball coach. I said, "It's okay, Coach, I forget things all the time and I'm not in my 90s."

Chapter 12:
A Presidential Honor

I was at the Coach's home not long after he received the Presidential Medal of Freedom from George W. Bush at the White House in 2003.

Of course, the Coach was typically modest in discussing the award, as if it wasn't a big deal. He said he enjoyed the trip very much, but I think he was afraid if he said too much, it would come off as bragging.

Coach gave a lot of credit to a former player, Andre McCarter, for spearheading a three-year campaign that led to the award. Coach was fond of McCarter, who was a key member of the 1975 championship team. That team, of course, was the last one ever coached by John Wooden.

This was a brief visit. I was mainly there to pick up a couple of autographed basketballs for an upcoming charity event.

My next visit with him was over dinner at a deli in the San Fernando Valley. I had arranged for my friend Victor Reskin to meet the Coach, and I invited my father to join us as well.

We talked for several hours, and Victor, in particular, was thrilled to talk about coaching his children in youth basketball.

One of the reasons he wanted to have dinner with Coach was to seek his advice.

At that age, Coach emphasized, the most important thing is that your players are having fun. "Don't do drills for more than 5 to 10 minutes," he told Victor.

Another dinner-table topic was Coach's hip problems. He had hip replacement surgery 15 years earlier in 1988, and now the hip was bothering him.

He said he had consulted a surgeon about the idea of another surgery, one in which the prosthesis would be replaced. The Coach said in all likelihood the surgeon would not do it.

"He feels that I'm too old, and as long as I can get by without surgery he would just as soon not do it," the Coach said.

Besides hearing of the hip pain Coach was suffering, it was a pleasant evening. It gave me great pleasure that I was able to arrange for my friend Victor to spend time talking with this legendary man.

During my next visit to Coach's condo to treat his feet, I had a chance to talk more about my upcoming charity event for Upward Bound House, the non-profit that provides shelter and skill training for impoverished families.

The Coach asked me what I needed besides signed basketballs. I told him I could use some more autographed copies of his Pyramid of Success. Of course he obliged. Before I left I told the Coach I would be seeing him soon.

A week later, it was late afternoon and I had just finished seeing my last patient. I double-checked with my assistant that she had confirmed Coach Wooden's appointment for that afternoon.

I packed my black bag with the necessary tools and headed to his home. As I drove up the 405 Freeway toward Encino, my thoughts were of Coach Wooden. As usual, I was excited about seeing him. It was almost as if I were the patient and he was the doctor.

After arriving at his home, we walked into his bedroom where the massage table was located at the foot of his bed. He sat at the edge of the table and took off his shoes and socks. I examined him and treated his feet.

We talked some more about the importance of taking care of one's feet. He reiterated that at the first practice each year he told his players how to put on their socks. He said he wanted to make sure there were no wrinkles. This, he said, reduced the chance of getting blisters.

He admitted to me that he knew most of his players thought these lectures on the correct way of putting on socks were silly.

After finishing my treatment on this day, I carefully watched as the Coach slowly and meticulously put his socks and shoes back on.

Then I drifted over to the study. As I sat down, the phone rang. I asked the Coach if he wanted me to answer it.

"No, let the answering machine get it," he said.

I think the answering machine was the only modern piece of equipment he had. Coach didn't have any fax machines, microwaves or large-screen televisions. He was certainly old school.

This call came from Gary Cunningham, who served as an assistant coach during the Wooden regime and later as UCLA's head coach. Of course Coach picked up the phone and they had a pleasant conversation.

The Coach never had a huge staff like today's college coaches have. As this is written, current UCLA Coach Steve Alford has seven assistants. John Wooden had two assistants when he first came to UCLA, although both were part-time. Ed Powell, who came with the Coach from Indiana State and had played for him at South Bend Central High School, was also the assistant baseball coach. Bill Putnam, a holdover from the Wilbur Johns era, was also the school's lone assistant athletic director.

Coach Wooden told me his assistants spent a lot of time making sure the players were doing well academically. In particular, he cited Crum and Cunningham.

"They each had a Ph.D. in education," the Coach said. "They would spend time observing the players in class and then speak with their professors. Both were concerned that all our players were doing well in their studies."

As I have mentioned before, Coach Wooden, in our conversations, always spoke of individuals in a positive way. Of course I never prodded him for anything negative. My job was not that of a hard-hitting, investigative reporter.

The Coach seemed to live by the motto, "If you can't say anything nice about someone, don't say anything at all."

So did my father. He made friends wherever he went because he was kind to everyone.

Coach and my father were also very family oriented. Helping family members came naturally to them, and it was always a priority.

One time when I was returning home from podiatry school in Cleveland my plane was scheduled to land at 3 a.m. I planned to grab a cab to get home. But when I walked from the plane into the terminal, there was my dad. I was stunned, particularly since it was a cold, rainy night.

"You didn't have to come and pick me up," I told him.

"I woke up at 2 a.m. and couldn't get back to sleep," he said with a shrug, as if it were no big deal.

We hugged before heading to his car. I could imagine Coach Wooden doing something like that for a family member.

Chapter 13:
The Coach, James Arness and Poetry

I've mentioned before that the walls in the Coach's condo were filled with photos. There was one wall in his bedroom dedicated to photos of family members—with one exception. It was a photo of James Arness, the actor who played Marshall Matt Dillon on the iconic television series *Gunsmoke*.

As I recall, it was the only photo not of a family member in the Coach's bedroom. The Coach explained that Arness was Nell's favorite actor.

Coincidentally, James Arness was also one of my patients.

The next time Arness came to my office, I mentioned the photo and explained how I knew about it. Arness said he was a great admirer of Coach and asked if there was any way he could meet him.

I told him I would work on that, and I did. I arranged a lunch meeting at VIP's for November 19, 2003, the date of my next scheduled appointment with Coach. The lunch would also include Arness' wife Janet.

When I visited Wooden's home that morning, he was in good spirits as I treated him. I think he was really looking forward to our lunch.

At lunch, I learned the Coach and Arness had met before. Arness' son Rolf had attended one of the Coach's basketball camps in the 1960s.

According to his father, Rolf Aurness (Aurness was James Arness' birth name) had potential as a basketball player, but he ended up starring in surfing. In 1970, at the age of 18, the curly-haired Rolf Aurness won that year's World Surfing Championships, which were held in Australia.

Our lunch went well. Arness told us things about himself that I didn't know. It was interesting for me to learn more about his life.

Arness, who died in 2011 at the age of 88, was originally from Minneapolis. He said he was not a good student, often skipping classes and barely graduating from high school. His early jobs included being a courier for a wholesale jeweler and working the freight yards, loading and unloading boxcars.

Arness told us he came to Los Angeles on a lark. A friend was going to Hollywood to audition for a movie and he invited him to come along. Arness was more interested in going to the beach to try surfing, but first he went with his friend to the audition.

While he stood to the side during the audition, the director noticed Arness and offered him a job in the movie as an extra. That was his start in the film industry.

I asked Arness how he ended up playing Matt Dillon on *Gunsmoke*, and he said John Wayne, who had turned down the role, recommended him for the job. I also learned that his younger brother is Peter Graves, who took his mother's maiden name. Graves, you may recall, starred in the TV series *Mission Impossible*.

I enjoyed seeing James Arness in a setting outside my office, and I think the Coach also appreciated our session with the actor.

During my next visit to the condo, the Coach and I talked about Pauley Pavilion. I asked him about the north and south baskets. I wanted to know why there was so much space between the crowd and the baskets, which was the case before the arena was remodeled. In other college arenas the crowd is very close to the basketball floor, but the Coach didn't want that to be the case at Pauley Pavilion. He thought that having the crowd so close to the court gave the home team an unfair advantage.

He also believed that the locker rooms should be the same for the home and visiting team. The visitors' locker room in Pauley Pavilion at the time still had metal lockers. The Coach said, "It's no better than a high school locker room."

Conversely, he said UCLA's home locker room had a lavish carpeted interior. "It was far superior," he said. He did not like that because he felt that when he was playing away from home, he wanted to be treated just the same as the home team. He felt that both locker rooms should be the same.

It should be noted that in the renovated Pauley Pavilion, which reopened in 2012, both locker rooms are plush.

The Coach and I spoke about his son Jim, and I asked if he thought it was difficult for Jim to live in the shadow of his father. The Coach said that he never put pressure on his son and never expected him to play basketball; however, he always supported him when he decided not to play basketball.

He said his son was a good basketball player at University High and probably could have gotten a Division I scholarship had he not hurt his knee in his senior season.

Somehow we started talking about hitchhiking, something Wooden often did during his high school and college days. During summers, he and his friends would hitchhike around the state looking for farm work. They would stay at farmhouses and sometimes be gone for weeks at a time. One time, he and a friend hitched all the way to South Dakota for a job.

While at Purdue, he often hitchhiked home from West Lafayette.

"You always got picked up," he said. "And you were never worried about it. It wasn't considered dangerous at all."

The Coach's farm work was largely responsible for his physique. As old photos show, it was impressive. He was muscular, yet trim and fit. And he was flexible, earning him the nickname "Indiana Rubber Man."

His physique was natural. The Coach never believed in weight training, either for himself or his players.

"Things have changed," he admitted.

Of course no visit with the Coach at his home was complete until he read some poetry. I can't say my level of enthusiasm for poetry was anywhere near the Coach's, but we did share a common interest in books. The Coach gave me many books over the years. Sometimes after treating him we would discuss them. In addition, he would always be generous in giving me new biographies that were written about him. However, he always would add: "Only read this if you have an interest."

Chapter 14:

Regrets, Imperfections and Sorrow

Although I have put the Coach on a pedestal, I realize no human being is perfect, or leads a perfect life. We all have our regrets, our imperfections and difficult periods of sadness.

I once asked the Coach about his regrets, and he mentioned two: Not treating the reserves better, and not traveling more with Nell.

Several of Coach's former reserve players had voiced complaints about lack of playing time. Coach did confide to me that when his teams were up by as many of 30 or 40 points, he probably should have played his reserves more. He claimed the reserves practiced hard and deserved playing time. He said he liked to have his top seven or eight players get as many minutes as possible.

Coach said he explained that philosophy to his reserves at the beginning of each season. But that did not appease many of them, and some players let their feelings be known.

One of those disgruntled players was Andy Hill, who documented his disappointments and hurt feelings in his 2001 book. Nearly 30 years after his playing days, Hill was reminded of his former coach while playing golf and his playing partner offered this advice: "Don't hurry, get your balance." That evoked the Wooden maxim: "Be quick, but don't hurry."

Hill wrote in his book that he found an old phone number for Coach in an address book and nervously dialed it. The number, to Hill's surprise, was still good. He got this message: "Hello, this is John Wooden. Please speak slowly and distinctly, and leave your name and number after the tone."

Hill wrote this about his reaction when hearing the message: "Hey, this wasn't so hard. I'll just leave word that I called."

But Coach picked up the phone and seemed generally excited to hear from his former player. After Coach invited Hill to come to his home for a visit, Hill asked the Coach to suggest a day and time.

"Right now would be fine," Coach said.

The two ended up becoming the best of friends.

Coach with Andy Hill

As for imperfections, it's known that Coach had a temper. However, he wasn't one to curse. "Goodness gracious sakes alive" was his way of cursing. He was taught not to curse by his father.

As a young boy growing up on the farm near Centerton, he and his older brother Maurice were in the barn when Maurice picked up a pitchfork and flipped manure at Coach's face. A fight broke out, which was witnessed by their father, Hugh. Both boys got a whipping, but Coach got the worst of it because he had cursed. It was a lesson well learned.

As for not traveling more with Nell, Coach claimed he wished he could have taken her to Europe and other areas of the world. Initially it was work that got in the way, then it was various commitments and obligations.

Nell died on March, 21, 1985.

Of the many books written about Coach, two were by Jay Carty, a former Oregon State basketball star and later coach. He was also an assistant coach under Gary Cunningham for the UCLA freshmen when Alcindor was on the team. In one of Carty's books, *Coach Wooden: One-On-One*, the Coach speaks of the loss of his beloved Nell, the biggest sorrow in his life.

Nell went into the coma after suffering a heart attack during hip replacement surgery in 1982. But on this occasion she rallied. After three months, Coach was able to take her home. "After 91 days in a complete coma, my wife Nellie squeezed my hand, opened her eyes and had a wonderful expression on her face that I can still see in my mind's eye," Coach is quoted as saying.

On Christmas Eve of 1984, the whole family, including Nell, gathered at Nan's house. "Nellie was happy," Coach says. "We had a nice evening."

But later that evening, she slipped back into a coma and never totally came out of it.

"We had been married for 53 years," Coach says. "She was the only girl I ever dated. It took me over two years to get past her death. I've never gotten over it."

Chapter 15:

Meeting Coach's First All-American

I continued to visit Coach's home to treat his feet on a regular basis, but as we grew closer, we didn't always discuss the past and his coaching career. Often, it was just small talk, and it often was more about what I was doing than about Coach.

Among the many things I admired about him was that he always showed interest in the person he was talking with. He always asked questions. In my case, he always asked about my family, in particular about my father and daughter, whom he had previously met.

During one of my summer visits to the condo, George Stanich was there. He was the Coach's first All-American, a carryover from the Wilbur Johns era.

The season before Wooden's arrival at UCLA, with the 6-foot-3 Stanich playing center, the Bruins finished 12-13. They were picked to finish last in their conference the next season.

Before the season Wooden had Stanich, his best player, switch to guard. The Coach also instilled a new work ethic, and the Bruins ended up finishing first in their division.

I enjoyed meeting and talking with George Stanich. He was a fascinating man, and a great all-around athlete. In the summer of 1948, prior to Coach's arrival at UCLA, Stanich won a bronze medal in the high jump at the London Olympics.

The spring of that year, Stanich was the star pitcher on the UCLA baseball team. The highlight of the season was a 2-0 shutout of USC, which ended up winning the 1948 College World Series.

Stanich was a contemporary of Hall of Famer Bill Sharman, an All-American in basketball at USC who also starred in baseball. Of Stanich's prowess in basketball, Sharman once said: "He was probably the toughest player I had to play against. He was faster and quicker and stronger than me."

In 1950, Stanich was drafted by the Rochester Royals of the fledgling NBA, winners of the league championship a year later, but signed a minor league baseball contract instead. However, baseball didn't work out.

"Baseball was where the money was," he said, "but things didn't work out. I got my head knocked off. They got to me, and they got to me good. The harder I tried, the worse it got."

Years later, Stanich did Coach—and UCLA—a big favor. He mentioned another outstanding all-around athlete, and pushed the Coach to recruit him. That athlete was a multi-sport star at El Segundo High. His name was Keith Erickson, and he became a key player on the Coach's first two national championship teams and a member of the 1964 U.S. Olympic volleyball team. He also became one of Coach's all-time favorite former players.

Keith Erickson

After Stanich left the condo, the Coach elaborated on his former player's all-around athletic ability and his success in the high jump as an Olympian. That led to a discussion about the Olympics in general. "I don't like the professionalism we now have in the Olympics," the Coach said. "Professional athletes should not be competing in the Olympics."

Religion was another topic on this day. I asked if a Jewish player had ever asked to miss practice on a Saturday, the Jewish Sabbath. The Coach said he didn't think that had ever happened.

He was opposed to Sunday games, although UCLA did have to play Notre Dame on a few Sundays because of television.

When I asked the Coach about his favorite trips, he told me about going to New Zealand in the mid-1950s to teach basketball. He was there for three months and enjoyed the countryside and the people. He said he spent a memorable week in one small village.

"The schoolhouse had only eight or nine students, and one teacher," the Coach said. "The students were all of different ages and grades, and the teacher had to come up with a curriculum that fit them all.

"The students were very obedient, and the teacher told me just about all of his students went to college."

I'm sure this reminded Wooden of his early days when he went to school in with multiple grades in a schoolhouse.

Before I left the Coach's home, Bill Walton called again during one of his bike rides on Coronado. He said he had a new bike, and raved about it.

"I'm happier than a pig in slop," Walton said.

Chapter 16:
Helping a Friend Deal with a Loss

My next visit was on October 15, the day after the Coach's 94th birthday. I brought along my oldest friend, Mark Fox. Mark's mother had just passed away and I was hoping to pick up his spirits.

It worked, and we had a wonderful time. Swen Nater was there, and that was a big plus. It was Swen who greeted us at the door.

Before I could sit down and chat, I needed to work on the Coach's feet. He told me that his spirits had been good and he was feeling fine but his toenails felt like talons, or curved claws.

After the Coach and I finished our business, we went into the living room to join Swen and Mark. The first thing we discussed was religion. The Coach said that he never pushed any type of religion on any of his players, but he thought it was important that his players had some kind of faith.

The Coach recalled a bus ride from South Bend, Indiana, to Chicago early in the 1968-69 season. It was during this bus ride that Lew Alcindor, then a senior, first revealed he had converted to Islam. He had read the autobiography of Malcolm X after his freshman year and had become intrigued. He studied at a mosque in Harlem during the summer of 1968, which prompted the conversion.

Listening most intently to Alcindor's admission was Steve Patterson, a born-again Christian, Terry Schofield, a Catholic, Don Saffer, who is Jewish, and Coach, a traditional Christian. Coach said it was overall a civil discussion, and worthwhile.

My friend Mark then spoke about his mother and how he was able to see her and sit with her the last couple of moments of her life. Mark said he held his mother's hand as she was passing.

Coach said he did the same for his wife and she would always be a part of him. The Coach spoke about his own mortality and said that he is not afraid to die. He said he did not want to die now, as he will miss his family and many friends and the people he has been with, but he said, "I look forward to the time when I will be with my Nellie up in heaven."

He had just celebrated a birthday with family and friends, and that had made him appreciate what he called a very full life. He said he had received more than 65 happy birthday wishes on his answering machine.

Toward the end of this visit, Swen Nater read a few of his poems.

Below is one I wrote for the Coach for his birthday.

TO MY PATIENT

I push the button where the elevator lies
And out comes my friend, with his kind blue eyes
He is always cheerful when we meet
You see I'm here to treat his feet

I go to his room with my black bag in hand
He removes his socks to be placed on the stand
My friend sits on his table and I check his skin
His pulses are sharp like the edge of a pin

I check his feet to be sure they are strong
You see my friend is busy all day long
He slowly pulls his socks up straight
And he always preaches, "Don't be late."
He ties his shoes and laces them tight
At ninety-two he still has some fight

We walk to his study with all its lore
I sit and listen, which is never a bore
The words he speaks I love to hear
The time we spend to me is dear

I take my jacket and bag from his rack
I hug my friend with a pat on his back
I again look forward to the time we meet
You see, I'm the doctor who takes care of his feet

Chapter 17:

A Different Kind of Water Shortage

By now it was 2005, and the Coach often appeared frail when I visited. One time when he asked for a glass of water, it prompted a story.

"You know, Dr. Levi, I limited my players to two sips of water during our practices," he said. "That was the thinking back then. It was how I was trained when I played, so that's what I did. Looking back now, it wasn't very bright of me."

He said he was sure many of his players didn't follow his rule to the letter of the law and would sneak in a few drinks of water.

I asked if he ever had a player pass out during practice or suffer from dehydration. He said he couldn't remember any specific problems due to a lack of water.

Coach told me he has recently suffered a considerable loss of blood and was sent to a hospital where he got a transfusion of four pints. However, that didn't keep him from a speaking engagement the next day.

I asked why he didn't cancel the lecture.

"I already had to cancel once several months prior and felt guilty about cancelling twice in a row," he said.

Even though the Coach didn't look good, he was lucid and never seemed to miss a joke.

It was his son Jim's birthday, so the Coach talked about him for a bit. Then the subject turned to his daughter Nan, who had just undergone shoulder-replacement surgery. The Coach was concerned about her, particularly since she already had both hips and a knee replaced.

Nan and her daughter Kathleen Trapani took care of the Coach, as did trainer Tony Spino and several of the Coach's former players. Kenny Washington often served as his driver but the Coach always declined Nan's offer for her or someone to move in.

"I never want to be a burden on anyone," he told me.

During another visit, Coach was entertaining a group of high school basketball players. He seemed to enjoy signing autographs and talking to the young men.

After they left, I treated him. Then we went to his study and had some time to talk. I asked him if he thought he could coach in today's world of college basketball. He said he thought he could, but he didn't think he could coach in today's world of professional basketball.

"Professional players these days are being paid so much money, they may not be interested in listening to a teacher," he said. "And I am a teacher."

The Coach's life path almost took a different route. He might have ended up as an English teacher rather than a teacher of basketball.

Coach went to Purdue hoping to get a degree in civil engineering, but that would require a summer internship, and he needed to do farm work the entire summer to make money. Around that time, he developed a relationship with the head of Purdue's English department, along with a love for the written word. He soon changed his major to English.

When he was at South Bend Central High, he not only coached basketball but also taught English. He enjoyed both very much.

Years later, while serving in the Navy, he got a number of letters from his former basketball players. But he rarely heard from any of his English students. This made him realize he had made a far greater impact as a coach than he had made as an English teacher.

"I loved to teach English, but you get closer to those under your supervision in sports than you do in the classroom," he said. "I can name almost all of the basketball players who played for me. I can't do the same for my English students."

That made sense to me, but I had never thought of it that way. That quotation illustrates the Coach's phenomenal memory. The fact that he could name almost all the basketball players who played for him didn't surprise me. Early on, I became aware of his ability to recall names and remember details. It was amazing.

Moving on to another topic, I asked the Coach if he was ever tempted to offer advice to any of the coaches who followed him at UCLA. The only one he mentioned was Jim Harrick, who guided UCLA to its only championship since the Coach's final one in 1975. Harrick's 1995 championship team featured the O'Bannon brothers, Ed and Charles, who were both left-handed.

"I mentioned to Jim a couple of times that he should utilize left-handed players to press," the Coach said. "But generally I stayed out of the way."

Chapter 18:
A Special Birthday Gift for My Dad

My father and I regularly had lunches together, usually twice a week. It was a tradition that began when I was in my early 30s. We also talked on the phone at least once a day.

After almost every phone call, I would sit back and wait a minute or so for his inevitable follow-up call, in which he would restate something we had just talked about or add a new thought. Our call-after-the-call would always make me smile; our little privately shared father-son idiosyncrasy.

Unfortunately, until I was 35, I had never realized how special my relationship with my father was. I simply thought all fathers and sons had the same intense and fulfilling bond we had. When I discovered its uniqueness, I rued my earlier lack of recognition.

We generally went to the same restaurant near my office in Santa Monica. The routine was always pretty much the same. My father would know our waitress or waiter's life story in a matter of minutes, like where he or she went to school, if they were married, or what his or her long-term goals were.

Sometimes, when the questioning went on awhile or I could see the server squirm a bit under the scrutiny, I would—like millions of children when they think that what their parents are doing something excessive—roll my eyes a bit. But servers never seemed to mind. They always found my father's inquisitions charming and friendly.

Another part of the routine was that he always ordered the same item, a chopped salad. "Chop it very finely," he would say. Then, again, as if the server hadn't heard him: "Chop it very finely." The response from the waiter or waitress, whether they had heard him the first time or not, was: "I know, Mr. Levi, chop the salad finely."

During lunch, he and I would talk about sports, my medical practice, business in general, the economy, gossip and, of course, family. Family was always at the center of his life.

After lunch, the server would bring the bill. My father always made it a point to tell the server how much he appreciated having his salad chopped very fine.

Often after our lunches, I did not want to go back to the office. Our time together was always so pleasant. But eventually we would hug and I slowly headed back to work.

One time when I returned to the office, I suddenly realized that my father's birthday was coming up soon. The perpetual dilemma smacked me in the head. How to celebrate? He was a man who never liked to make a fuss about his birthdays. His idea of a great birthday celebration was going out with the immediate family for a quiet dinner.

On his 50th and 75th birthdays, my sweet mother had pulled out all the bells and whistles. She invited all our friends and relatives to celebrate my dad's birthday with funny skits and monologues.

This birthday in 2006 was not one of those, however. It seemed like a quiet dinner was more appropriate. But where? As I went through my checklist of his favorite restaurants, I looked up and saw the perfect birthday present staring me in the face. It was a wonderful 11x16 picture of John Wooden, my dad and me taken some years earlier.

I called Coach Wooden at home and asked him if I could drop by his house in the next couple of days. I told him my father's birthday was coming up soon and I have a picture of the three of us I'd like him to sign.

He said: "What are you doing now?" It was 6 p.m.

"Just some paperwork and patient charting," I replied.

"Why don't you come right over?" he said. "As long as you don't mind that I'm in my pajamas."

I finished my charts and drove straight to the Coach's condominium. When I arrived, he was watching a World Series game between St. Louis and Detroit.

"After I sign the picture, would you like to stay and watch the game?" he asked.

There was no need to call my wife. I had already called to warn her that I was visiting Coach Wooden and likely would be late.

Coach signed the picture: "*Thank you, Mike Levi, for being 'snapped' with this ex-teacher coach and your son. Happy 75*th*, John Wooden UCLA.*"

Myron was my father's real first name, but he was known to everyone as Mike. So that was fine. And I didn't have the heart to tell Coach that it wasn't really his 75th birthday, that it was actually my father's 77th birthday.

This photo was my birthday gift to my father.

As we watched the game, Coach explained nuances I never knew existed. He was a true student of the game of baseball. The evening was magical. I did not want the game to end.

As I rose to leave, I said, "Thank you for the most wonderful evening."

"No, Dr. Levi, thank you—for both the visit and taking the time to come out. I always enjoy your company." With his eyes twinkling, he added, "And thank you for taking care of my feet."

As he escorted me to the door, he said, "Please wish your dad a happy birthday."

Several days later, on his birthday, I gave my dad his gift. As soon as he opened the wrapping and saw the autographed picture of us with the Coach, he smiled from cheek to cheek and told me how much he appreciated it. He got up from his chair, went to his study, and immediately put the framed picture on the wall.

The family went out for dinner and when we returned, my dad found a personal message on the answering machine. It was from Coach Wooden, wishing him a happy birthday.

Chapter 19:

Kareem and Coach Norman

When I visited the Coach in July of 2007, he told me his arthritis was acting up. He also said he had lost a lot of his appetite and had to force himself to eat. But this visit turned out to be a most interesting one. We first talked about Kareem Abdul-Jabbar delivering the UCLA commencement the previous month.

"I'm a little surprised he agreed to do it because he is such a quiet man," Coach Wooden said. "But I knew he would do well because he is very bright."

Coach and I had read some of the highlights of Kareem's speech, as reported in the media. Coach had particularly liked what his former player had said about success and how he had injected some humor in his speech.

"Success is pretty easy," Kareem had told the graduates. "Here's a hoop, here's a ball; you put the ball through the hoop—that's success."

Kareem Abdul-Jabbar, the NBA's all-time leading scorer, added that he's called a success because he was able to "put the ball through the hoop more than anyone in history."

What's less appreciated, he pointed out, is that he worked tirelessly for 20 years to succeed.

Kareem had cited the insights of Albert Einstein and French novelist Gustave Flaubert to stress the importance of being worthy of success. Quoting Einstein, he said: "Try not to become a man of success, but rather become a man of value." He then quoted Flaubert, who once said: "Success is a result, not a goal."

"I'm not claiming that you have to sell all your worldly possessions, wander the globe in rags, or worse, cancel HBO," Kareem quipped. "You should embrace and celebrate your pleasures, but also prove that you are worthy of being successful by making yourself significant."

As we discussed Kareem's performance, I could tell Coach was very proud of him.

Coach said he was going to have breakfast with Bill Walton in a few days, which was nothing unusual. But then he startled me with some shocking news.

Jerry Norman, the Coach's varsity assistant from 1958 through 1968, a man often credited with building the foundation for the UCLA basketball dynasty, had just called him. Norman would be coming to the Coach's home for a visit in 11 days. The date would be July 17, 2007.

The Coach was amazed he had called. He said the two had barely spoken since Norman had walked away from his job at UCLA in 1968.

There had been some conjecture at the time that Norman's salary of only $14,000 was one reason he left. But Coach's salary was only $17,000 at the time. Another reason for Norman's departure, some reasoned, was that Coach had not given him enough credit for helping build the UCLA dynasty. "I don't think we've spoken in 35 years," the Coach told me. "I'm very curious about what he has to say."

The next time I saw the Coach, several months later, I forgot to ask him how the lunch with Jerry Norman had gone.

Norman, contacted by phone while in the process of writing this book, said, "We just talked about old times and a lot of our memories. It was a very pleasant. After lunch he invited me back to his condo to sit and talk some more.

"I just decided that since he was getting up in years, that I should call him and we should talk. That was all there was to it. It was just the right thing to do."

Chapter 20:
The Final Chapter

I went to Coach's home on Wednesday, November 27, 2007, at one o'clock in the afternoon. I rang the doorbell and no one answered. I waited for what seemed like another 15 minutes, but again no one came to the door.

I called the Coach's house phone and no one answered.

At 1:30, I called his daughter Nan and asked her if her father was expecting me. She said he was, and immediately came over.

We rang the doorbell and no one answered. We opened the door and the room was dark. His bedroom door was closed. We opened the door and saw him sleeping away in his bathrobe.

Coach had been ill the whole week with a bad case of flu. He was very weak. In spite of that, he wanted me to treat his feet. Afterwards, we sat and talked for awhile. We had hot chocolate and some crackers and talked about the upcoming holidays.

His health had gone downhill in the previous six months. When I would see him, he seemed to almost always have a bad cold. He was not attending UCLA basketball games. However, even as his health declined, his spirit remained intact and he was lucid.

I did not see Coach again until January 6, 2008. Tony Spino had spent the night. Again, the Coach had a bad cold and was weak. And again, he wanted to be treated.

His granddaughter, Caryn Bernstein, was also at his home. She lived nearby and was there to help care for her grandfather while also cleaning his place and organizing his many mementos. Coach was something of a packrat, and there were letters everywhere throughout the small condo.

After I finished treating Coach's feet, I invited him to my son's bar mitzvah. He said he had attended several bar mitzvahs in the past. I told him he would receive an invitation and I hoped he would come.

I knew it was doubtful he could, particularly because his health was declining and his ability to get places was becoming more difficult.

While we were talking, he spoke about Caryn's daughter Cori, Coach's first great-granddaughter, who was in the process of getting a teaching credential. Coach said that at one time she was interested in medicine, but had decided that a career in teaching better suited her.

In January of 2009, I went to visit Coach Wooden at a rehabilitation facility. He had undergone surgery on a hand that had been bothering him. He seemed happy to see me, although he looked tired. He didn't complain about any pain, but then he never did.

His great-granddaughter Cori was there. She had just landed a teaching position in Riverside, and was going be married in July. She would then be Cori Anderson.

Nan and Jim were also there. They were concerned about their father, particularly now that his spirits were low.

I could identify with what Nan and Jim were going through. It had been six months since my father had been diagnosed with pancreatic cancer. My situation in dealing with my father was similar to theirs, yet there were differences as well. Coach appeared to be accepting of the end. My father didn't want to be a burden to his friends or anyone else, but he was frustrated and wanted to continue to live, no matter how grave his situation became.

I tried to keep my father engaged in my life, seeking his advice, be it something to do with my work, my family, a friend, or an acquaintance. He would often call and I think it helped him feel more alive. Unfortunately the calls became more and more difficult, as toward the end they often came in the middle of the night.

When my father succumbed to cancer on March 23, 2010, it was the saddest day of my life.

***

Several weeks later, I decided to bring my mother Ursula to the Coach's home. She had met him at benefits and charitable functions, but had not spent much time with him. She was reluctant to visit his home, particularly since she knew his health was deteriorating. I convinced her to go. When we arrived at his home, he was sitting in his chair in the living room. He seemed happy to meet my mother again. He asked about my dad and gave his heartfelt condolences.

However, I felt that the Coach was going downhill quickly. It was obvious that he had lost the will to live. His conversations were shorter than usual. In addition, it seemed that he was always tired.

I saw Coach one more time, a few days before his death on June 4, 2010 at the Ronald Regan UCLA Medical Center. He had been there for a week and had asked me to come by since time was dwindling.

When I arrived, I was given his room number, as he was listed under an anonymous name.

When I went to his bedside, he seemed peaceful. The chaplain was in the other room talking to Nan. I touched Coach's forehead and his eyes opened and he had a smile. He said hello and that he appreciated me coming by. He had not shaved in many days and looked scruffy.

He closed his eyes and I began to talk to him and I told him how much he meant to my father and me.

Some time passed and Bill Walton came in. Again, the Coach opened his eyes and said hello. Even in this time of quietness, he still seemed to have a zest for humor. As Coach rubbed his straggly beard, he looked at Bill and said, "I would never let you play with this." Then he closed his eyes again.

Nan told me of a similar story. Bill Sharman and his wife Joyce had also come to visit Coach. Joyce tried talking to Coach, but he was not responding.

Joyce then invited Nan to join her and Bill for dinner, adding, "And you can have a class of wine."

"Maybe two glasses," Nan said.

Suddenly, there was movement from the Coach, as he raised his hand and held up one finger. The hand went down and again the eyes were closed.

Nan was a bit startled, as were the Sharmans. "That's Daddy," Nan finally said. "He never let me have more than one glass of wine."

They all laughed.

Nan seemed to enjoy telling this story, explaining it added a little levity to the moment.

It was now time for me to leave. I kissed the Coach on the forehead, said my final goodbyes and slowly walked out of the room. I then went to Nan and gave her my best and biggest hug. I shed a tear knowing that I would never see my dear friend again. Then, as another tear trickled down my cheek, my thoughts were drawn to my father. I had been so fortunate to have both my father and Coach Wooden, two wonderful men, in my life.

Afterword

I had wanted to write this book since the passing of my father Mike and Coach Wooden a few months apart in 2010. My thinking was to pay tribute to both. They had similar values, which included always putting family first.

My father was always involved in my life. He let me make my own decisions, sometimes with not the most desirable results, but his unconditional love never wavered. Coach Wooden was much the same with his two children and their many offspring.

Both men also had the support of wonderful women. The Coach had Nell, whose influence never subsided following her death in 1985. My father had my mother Ursula, whose grace and unconditional love were paramount to my father's success. As this is written, I speak to my mother daily.

After the Coach passed, there was a large memorial held in Pauley Pavilion. Many dignitaries and former players attended, though I chose not to. As I wrote in the last chapter, I had said my goodbyes in the hospital, kissing his forehead and hugging his daughter.

In 2011, I began teaching a medical class at Loyola Marymount University. I annually dedicate one night to John Wooden. I begin the class by asking my students, "How many of you know of John

Wooden?" Usually only a few raise their hands. I then teach them about this great man and his Pyramid of Success and explain how the building blocks and quotations have affected my life.

On these nights, I also bring in a guest speaker, who is usually a former player for Coach Wooden. Guest speakers have included Kareem Abdul-Jabbar, Bill Walton, Swen Nater and Andy Hill. Another guest speaker was Craig Impelman, a former UCLA assistant coach who is married to Coach's granddaughter Christy.

The guest speakers talk about how Coach affected them not only during their college days but on through their adult lives. My hope is that during my students formative years they too, like me and so many others, can be inspired by the teachings of John Wooden.

Acknowledgements

Many people need to be thanked for the long hours of writing, rewriting, and research. Credit for much of the hard work goes to co-author Larry Stewart. He is wonderful to work with and I cherish our friendship. His wife Norma, an astute editor, and daughter Kelly, an excellent typist, helped make this book possible. I'm thankful for their endless hours of hard work. I would also like to thank Nan Wooden for her contributions and letting me present stories about her late father. Also, I'd like to thank my mother Ursula, who has influenced me throughout my life and has always supported me in all my endeavors. I'd also like to thank my father-in-law Harold Kuhn and my friend Cliff Osmond for their support with this project. Cliff was my co-author prior to his passing from pancreatic cancer in 2012.

Finally, I would like to thank my family, including my wife Lori and my children Rachel and Jonathan, for their encouragement over the years. They also listened to me talk ad nauseam about Coach Wooden. They knew how important this book was to me, and how much both my father and Coach Wooden influenced my life.

About the Authors

Besides having a podiatric practice in Santa Monica, California, Dr. Michael Levi finds time to provide his services elsewhere. He is the team podiatrist for the Los Angeles Clippers of the NBA, the Loyola Marymount University athletic department and the Los Angeles Ballet Company. He also volunteers at the L.A. Zoo, taking care of the podiatric ailments of the primates. In addition, he holds teaching positions at the Western College of Podiatric Medicine in Pomona and Loyola Marymount University in Los Angeles. Dr. Levi, who resides in West Los Angeles with his wife Lori, also participates in triathlons, including the Half-Ironman on the big island of Hawaii.

Co-author Larry Stewart was a sportswriter and editor in Los Angeles for nearly 40 years — nine at the old L.A. Herald Examiner and 30-plus at the L.A. Times. Stewart also had a close relationship with Coach Wooden and remains close with his daughter Nan.

Printed in Canada